RIVER OF TIME

. . . *Memories of a Life Well Lived*

Worley Faver

i

SeaDog Press, LLC
830 A1A North, Suite 13
Ponte Vedra Beach, Florida 32082

Contact seadogpressllc@gmail.com regarding inquiries.
Cover Design: SeaDog Press, LLC /
www.seadogpressllc.com
Palm Valley Bridge Painting: Joe Taylor, Artist
Cover Image: Jim Gray, Photographer
Ship Logo: © Dn Br | Shutterstock
Branch of Leaves: © Terbrana | Shutterstock
Great Blue Heron: © Nature Art | Shutterstock
Siamese Cat: © Serge 75 | Dreamstime
Running Horse: © onot | Shutterstock
Painted Swamp: © Vidux|Shutterstock

Introduction

My friend, Worley, calls this "a little book" of stories. It may be little in size but in feel and sensibility it is a universe. The stories reflect the aspects of his past and present and the future he already knows that have made him who he is. They paint the flow of the influences of his life, from the spirit of his 17th century ancestors who first settled in America to his certainty that after he leaves this plane, this incarnation, he will reconnect with all who went before and all who come after.

Worley's children, grandchildren, and friends begged for these stories to be written down. We have heard them in his speaking voice for as long as we have known him, but we needed the security of having them in written form to ensure we would remember their richness as our own journeys through this life grew longer.

These stories show the evolving Worley: the child and young man whose family and experience of the natural world shaped his future; the adult who came to understand the power of art and who is able to demonstrate it through his pottery; and the elder who senses the links between what has gone before and what will come.

Enjoy the journey of Worley Faver.

Emily Trapnell
Roanoke, Virginia
November, 2015

TO
MY FRIEND
ROBERT
ALL THE BEST

Worley

DEDICATION

Today I visited her, as I always do when I'm discouraged and
finding little success in bringing my "personal legend" to
reality. She does not lie under that tombstone in the grass, but
when I need to feel especially close to her, this is the place to
which I return. She lives in my blood and genes, but most of
all she lives in my spirit. My eyes have not looked upon her for
sixty-five years, but she never ever left my heart. In my
moments of physical and emotional pain, she has always been
there with her healing hands. Because of her, I know the
meaning of unconditional love and have, in my own small way,
been able to share that love with a few others. These words
are for you — my precious Grandmother.

ACKNOWLEDGMENTS

What a wonderful experience to have the opportunity to work with the best publisher and editor in the world of books. My publisher, Captain Garry Karsner, SC, USNR (Ret), and editor, Florence Love Karsner, made the whole writing process a pleasure for this old author. They displayed incredible patience, expertise, and untiring effort in helping me create these stories. It was truly a joy to be exposed to their intelligence and good humor. Without their encouragement and friendship this project would have been impossible.

CONTENTS

1

GRANDPA WILL (1867-1940)

Arrival in America

The Van der Groeft family arrived in New Amsterdam from Holland in 1657. As many immigrants before them, they "Americanized" their family name to DeGrove in 1750. The family prospered in their new home up until the Revolutionary War. Our cousin, Rachel, married an Englishman and was designated "tainted" by the new American Government and forced to flee to Canada after the Revolution.

According to family records the DeGroves owned property on Manhattan Island in an area which they described as "swampy land." Today that land is under 33 Wall Street and the J.P. Morgan building. They also owned part of Pier 3 on the Hudson River. The land on Wall Street was lost in a long complicated law suit, 1832-1839. The Hudson River property was not lost. This was the beginning of the DeGrove family in America.

Florida

My grandfather, William Morton DeGrove, arrived in North Florida in 1873 when he was seven years old. The name of the village was Fruit Cove on the St. Johns River, where his father planted citrus and other fruit trees. His father, William, had been a telegraph superintendent during the early days of telegraphy in Kentucky.

In less than eight years his mother, father, and twin brothers had died. The killer was probably influenza. An aunt who taught school in Clay County helped raise the remaining children. Her name was Fredonia, but in our family this angel has always been known as "Aunt Donie." In his early twenties, Will met and married Mary Townsend who was raised in west Jacksonville. Only one story from that courtship survives.

It has been said that when Grandpa first saw Mary at a dance, it was love at first sight. Apparently he and his friends were sipping from their flasks and when his friends saw his attraction to Mary, they dared him to wash his coat in the punch bowl. After he ruined his coat and the punch, we wonder what sort of impression this made on my grandmother, who was a very quiet and beautiful girl.

Palm Valley

The little village was called Diego. In the early 1600's the Spanish army and a few settlers built a small wooden fort called Fort San Diego. This was an early warning outpost to protect St. Augustine from English invaders from Georgia and to protect them from Indian raids.

In 1895 Grandpa bought seventy-two acres of land in Diego for $300. We think he had received some money from the sale of Pier 3 on the Hudson River. He and his surviving brother and sisters were the only living heirs of William Michael DeGrove. Pier 3 sold in 1896 for $85,000. Will and his bride, Mary, built a small house on the property and commenced building a large stone and cypress two-story home. When completed in 1910, their home was called "The Big House" by the neighbors. This is the house I grew up in and it still stands today.

Will and Mary raised seven children in that house, Edward, John, Charley, Doris, Marie, Russell, and my mother, Birdie. Soon after moving into The Big House, Grandpa persuaded the few settlers in Diego to change the name of the community to Palm Valley.

When I moved into The Big House in 1940 the names of the neighbors close by, not related to our family in Palm Valley, were Mickler, Henson, West, and Mier. The property had a large sugar cane field west of the house, where the best cane syrup I ever tasted was created. There were pecan, persimmon, orange, fig, and pear trees, as well as a peach orchard and grape arbors. There were two varieties of orange trees (one for juice and eating fresh and the other for marmalade) and two varieties of grapes (one for jelly and one for eating fresh).

When the sugar cane was harvested in the fall, the field was left to rest until Uncle Charlie planted the spring/summer garden, where all of our fresh vegetables were produced. We never bought vegetables because Granny and Mama canned enough in the summer to last through the winter. The peach trees bloomed in February and the fruit was harvested in June. I can still taste that homemade, hand-churned, peach ice cream.

East of the house was the "big field," where

produce was grown to sell to Mr. Crowe's grocery store, the only one in Jacksonville Beach. Grandpa and his sons grew sweet potatoes, pole beans, and other large crop vegetables in the big field.

Here's a story about the big field I have to tell. One day I was driving a tractor pulling the harrows and preparing the soil for the next crop when I heard one of the harrow blades strike something hard. Getting off the tractor I found that I had run over a bottle, without breaking it. Wiping the bottle off, I found it was filled with a clear liquid. When I swirled the bottle around, beads rose from the bottom. I knew I had found something special. At the end of the day I drove over to Flavian Mickler's house. He inspected the bottle, then pulled the cork to sniff the contents. He smiled and said, "William, this is a special vintage and we can't let it go to waste," so we sat in the afternoon shade and enjoyed the best moonshine we would ever drink.

Grandpa Will earned his living as a farmer and mail-carrier. He served on the St. Johns County Commission from 1902 through 1910 and was elected to the Florida Legislature in 1916 where he served two terms. The second run for election produced a very nice "left handed" compliment from his opponent who said, "Will DeGrove is the meanest man in Palm Valley, but he is also the most honest."

While in Tallahassee he sponsored bills to give women the right to vote (Women's Suffrage) and was also instrumental in dividing St. Johns County to create Flagler County. I have an old photograph of my grandmother and my mother (all dressed up in a long white dress with matching hair ribbon), probably made in Tallahassee during a legislative session. They would board the train at Pablo (later Jacksonville Beach) to travel to Tallahassee.

In the early days the state of Florida was divided into two counties with Escambia County in the far western part of the state and St. Johns County covering the rest. Grandpa's help in dividing St. Johns County finally brought the area of the county to a reasonable size. This final division of the county created Flagler County.

Family legend also says that he supported the idea to clean up the St. Johns River in the area of Jacksonville where raw sewage was contaminating the water. I imagine this idea may have come from Uncle Henry who was Captain on the St. Johns River Dayline Steamer "Magnolia."

One afternoon Grandpa was sitting on the front porch resting from the daily toil when he noticed a man running up the lane to The Big House. When the man reached the porch out of breath and visibly very frightened, Grandpa asked him what was wrong. The man said, "Mister Will, you are the only person who can save me. I'm a Minorcan from St. Augustine. I'm being chased by the Ku Klux Klan because of an untrue trumped-up charge." Sure enough, up the lane came several men dressed in the white robes of the KKK. Grandpa calmly moved the Minorcan to stand behind him and called his boys out of the house.

The leader of the KKK said, "Mr. DeGrove you have to turn this Minorcan over to us to be punished." Grandpa said, "Gentlemen, if you want him, you will first have to go through me and my sons." The Klan backed down that day. There was no violence and the Minorcan was returned safely to his family.

How I wish I had known my Grandpa Will. I was only three when he died in his seventy-fourth year. Thankfully, I can still remember his face. He apparently was one of those larger-than-life, "force-of-nature" men.

He divided his property between his children, set aside land for a family cemetery, and donated a fairly large tract to the Palm Valley Baptist Church, where he was a leader and deacon. He also offered land to the U.S. Government to be used as a post office.

His oldest son, Edward, died of tuberculosis when he was twenty eight.. Grandpa did everything he could to save him. According to family legend, he even sent him to New Mexico for treatment in the dry climate.

My mother was the "baby" in the family and could have been his favorite. She was born May 9, 1910. Her name was Birdie and he called her his "little May bird."

Apparently no alarm clock was needed in The Big House. My mother said that every morning Grandpa would go to the kitchen and while putting the coffee on, that old Baptist hymn "When the Roll is Called Up Yonder," was sung loud enough to wake the entire household.

One morning in 1940, my dear grandmother woke up and found him lying beside her very still and not breathing. He went to the other side while in his sleep. What a wonderful way to leave this world. His passing was recognized by the Florida Legislature in House Resolution #39, which honored him as a "pioneer of Florida and a man of exemplary character and Christian faith."

After he left, my mother moved our family into The Big House so that Granny would not have to live alone. After we moved, I enjoyed the perfect childhood, spoiled to perfection by my granny and my mother. There are so many happy memories and if I dream of a house to this day, it is always The Big House.

At ten years old I roamed the woods around the house to shoot squirrels, which Granny would fry for supper. If the sun went down before I came from the woods, Mama would step out on the back porch and call me. There was also some sadness.

Playing on the front porch one day, I noticed two messages written in pencil on the stone wall of the house. They were alike except the names. Here is what they said: "Remember Edward (John) Degrove." Both of these uncles died in The Big House from tuberculosis. Eddie was twenty eight and John was in his late forties, I believe.

What a wonderful example Grandpa Will was, showing us how to live and love.

*

Grandpa Will circa 1890 — age 27

DeGrove Family at the Big House — circa 1935

*Mary Townsend DeGrove (My Grandmother) and
Mary Birdie DeGrove (My Mother)*

2

MULLET ON THE BEACH

In the 1940s in Palm Valley, when October and November rolled around, we all looked forward to hearing someone shout, "mullet on the beach."

The adult mullet would swim up the St. Johns River during the warm summer to spawn. The babies hatched and grew during the warm weather and headed to the mouth of the river in the fall. They would spill out of the river by the millions. As soon as the migration started, our family began making plans for a wonderful beach outing — fried mullet on the beach.

In those days there was no electricity in Palm Valley. That lost art form — letter writing, was how families stayed in touch, so Mama and Granny would send letters to our relatives in Jacksonville spreading the news that mullet were on the beach. What great fun. I can remember from three years old onward how much our family enjoyed each other and the love they shared.

Uncle Charley would show up with his large cast iron frying pan, salt, pepper, a bag of cracker meal and a large coffee pot. Mama would bring one of her famous jelly cakes, the one with 5 layers and homemade grape jelly between the layers.

Only a couple of cast nets were needed because the mullet were passing by just behind the breakers enmasse moving from north to south and one cast sometimes caught so many fish that the net had to be dragged to the beach. The mullet were cleaned in the surf, salt and peppered, shook in a bag of cracker meal and placed in the hot bacon grease. No fish has ever tasted that good to me.

After the family fish fry, the men turned to fishing at night to catch fish for the market. When I was ten or eleven years old, I remember one special night of fishing with the men of our family. Bubba Mickler and I were usually on the lead staff of the long seine, which was over a hundred feet long. This was well before the days of monofilament webbing, which is waterproof, strong, and light. Our net was probably cotton mesh or possibly nylon, which was a new invention back then.

Anyhow, here is the scene. It's 2:00 A.M. and Bubba and I are chest deep behind the breakers pulling the seine from south to north around the mullet. Our net had the usual lead line at the bottom and cork line at the top, with about six feet of hand woven mesh between. It was black dark; the phosphorescence in the water would glow with every move.

A couple of the men on the beach would use their lit cigarettes to signal us to go deeper or move in a little and then at the end of the haul, signal to bring the end of the net into the beach. One of the men would hold the beach staff on the other end of the seine and move with us down the beach.

One night Bubba and I were up to our necks in the water pulling when the staff was almost pulled out of our hands as it shook violently. We immediately headed in to the beach and we all could not believe what we saw. Apparently, a large shark became entangled in the net and ripped out a section large enough to drive a car through.

There is real danger in the ocean. One day years later, I saw Flavian throw his cast net over a breaker and was almost drowned. The net had covered a very large tarpon in the surf, which caused the fish to spook and head out to deep water with Flavian and his net in tow. Somehow he was able to remove his hand from the loop of the hand line and swim back to shore. The cast net was lost but he was alive.

The mullet run was a source of income every year for the Palm Valley people. This was before there were 4-wheel drive vehicles available to the public. They were only used in the military in those days. The vehicle we drove the beaches with was usually a Model A Ford with a homemade, wooden, truck style body built on the back. After a night of seining, the body would be running over with mullet. The men would drive the mullet to the Jacksonville Beach ice house and receive two cents a pound for a hard night's work.

These are some wonderful memories now in my seventy-ninth year. Life was certainly not easy in those days, but the pace was more leisurely and uncomplicated.

I remember the gas lights in our house and sitting around a battery operated radio to listen to the news, The Lone Ranger, or maybe The Green Hornet. Every Friday night in the summer Daddy would bring home a pound of shrimp and we would fish in the intracoastal every Saturday morning. In the winter we would go in the woods every Saturday to gather fire wood for the two fireplaces in The Big House. All the wood was cut with a crosscut saw or axe. This was a long time before chainsaws.

Those days are long past, but I still remember the love and kindness of all those fine people.

*

Family Frying Mullet on the Beach

3

TO AMERICA

First, let me apologize for the beginning of this story, which starts on a very sad note indeed. In 1572 our family members were French Huguenots (French Calvinist Protestants). In August, 1572, they were victims of the St. Bartholomew massacre. Estimates of the French Huguenots killed by members of the Catholic faith range from 5,000 – 30,000. I once saw in some old family correspondence the following statement: "Today, Dr. William LeFevre and his son were killed because of their religion."

After this horrible event the letter stated, aristocrats, nobles, and the LeFevre family left France for Ireland. Almost two generations later, our family reached the shores of America. The family settled in Culpepper County, Virginia, in circa 1634. One of the first acts of the family in their new home was to change their name from LeFevre to Faver to forever disown them from France.

By the time of the Revolutionary War the Faver

family had migrated to Greenville in Meriwether County, Georgia. One family member, John Faver, was wounded during the battle of Kettle Creek (February 14, 1779), which is located in Wilkes County, Georgia.

A British force of 700 men under Colonel Boyd engaged an American force of 500 men under General Elijah Clark, Colonel Dooly of Georgia, and Colonel Pickens of South Carolina. The British were defeated and routed and Colonel Boyd was wounded and ultimately died on the battlefield.

This was not the only battle in which the Faver family participated during the birth of our nation. Because of their support, members of the family received grants of land. After the Revolution, family members were active in local politics and served as Justice of the Peace, Sheriff of Meriwether County, and the Georgia Legislature.

W. Reuben Faver was a farmer and owned more than 1,000 acres in Greenville, Georgia, in 1811. I have visited his grave which is located in the center of the original property. The grave site is deeded to the Faver family. One of Reuben's sons, William R. Faver, inherited the family farm and also served as Sheriff of Meriwether County prior to 1843. I was able to visit the red brick sheriff's office and jail, which still stand in downtown Greenville.

William married Mary Elizabeth Hall on June 29, 1843. Elizabeth's family had a history sadly similar to the Faver family. The Hall family came to America because of the persecution of Presbyterians by the Church of England in Scotland. William's oldest son was Alexander Columbus Faver and was my great grandfather. He was born July 17, 1844. People in our family today love to say that my first son, Keith, and I inherited Alexander's wildness, although Keith and I discount this. We say we just enjoy life to the fullest.

I guess from the stories that have come down through the years concerning Alexander, he really was "The Wild Man." I have read in our family genealogy that the people in Greenville used to love to sit in the courthouse square and watch Alexander arrive in town. Whether he was driving a team of horses behind a carriage/wagon or in the saddle, he would always make at least one circle around the square at breakneck speed.

Even as a teenager he was a master horseman. His father begged him to not volunteer for service in the War of Northern Aggression. As Sheriff, William could have had him excused from service. However, Alexander dreamed of serving in the Confederate Calvary, which he did. He came through the War without a scratch.

After the War, an event occurred which would change his life. While on a business trip to Atlanta, circa 1867, he and his two friends were stopped on the road by a band of armed men. Heated words were exchanged, pistols were drawn, and Alexander shot and killed one of the men, and quickly made his escape. Shortly, a posse arrived and tracked him, but he was not to be found. He had turned his horse loose and hid in the top of a tree all night.

After this incident, Alexander returned home for his wife Emma and they fled to Texas. During the journey, relatives in Alabama and Louisiana assisted the couple during their travel. They were welcomed by an uncle in Texas and lived there for over a year.

Then the unthinkable happened. An attorney, who was a friend of the family, went before a judge and argued that the killing was an act of self-defense by Alexander. The judge agreed and vacated the warrant against

Alexander.

There may be another reason for our wild genes. Milton Faver was born in Virginia in 1822. According to the Texas State Historical Association, Milton moved from Virginia to Missouri where as a young man he fought a duel and fled to Mexico.

He met and married a Mexican woman and eventually moved to the Big Bend country of Texas. He became one of the first Texas cattle barons.

Their military protection at Fort Davis was abandoned before the Civil War. Milton built his own headquarters and adobe fort in Cibolo as protection against Apache Indian raids. After the Civil War he owned over 10,000 cattle and almost 3,000 acres of land.

Alexander's second son, born January 10, 1871, was my Grandfather, Alexander Hall Faver. Unfortunately, I do not remember him as he died in 1938 and I was born in 1937. Hall Faver, as he was called, moved from Greenville, Georgia, to St. Augustine, Florida, as a grown man. He met and married Florida Ellen Dykes from Altoona, Florida, on May 30, 1899.

Here is an interesting story regarding my Grandmother's engagement ring. Grandfather Hall wanted to propose to Florida Ellen but needed to purchase an engagement ring.

One day while strolling through the court yard of the old Spanish Fort Castillo de San Marcos he noticed a hand protruding through the bars of the fort prison cell. (Note: During the United States Army campaign against the western Indian tribes, some captive warriors were sent to the St. Augustine fort for incarceration.) So Grandfather stepped closer to the bars and saw a ring in the hand of an Indian. They exchanged a few words, and this is how my Grandmother's engagement ring was purchased for $1.00.

The gold ring was beautiful, set with black natural pearls and an inset engraved amethyst. My grandmother loved it and wore it until she passed away from consumption (tuberculosis) on June 29, 1916.

The ring has led an interesting life. My Uncle Hiram, Grandmother's first son, born in 1900, inherited the ring when she passed away. He was St. Johns County's Clerk of the Circuit Court, and after he had been wearing the ring for a time, he thought he had lost it forever one day.

He was in Miami attending a Florida Sheriff's Conference and went into the rest room of the Court House. He left the ring on the lavatory after washing his hands. When he returned to St. Augustine and discovered the loss, he immediately called his friend, the Sheriff of Dade County. Deputies found the ring in a Miami pawn shop and returned it to Hiram.

He wore the ring for over sixty years, and then on his passing, his sister, my Aunt Elizabeth, placed it in a safety deposit box. Upon her passing, the ring passed to my cousin, Joan Sabol, and she gave it to her daughter, Patricia, who in turn passed it to my son, Keith. Keith loves to put the ring on his finger, tell the story and then show it to his friends. The story gets better after a couple of glasses of wine.

My Grandfather Faver was an interesting man. He owned The Ancient City Wagon Works before automobiles took over the streets. People used horses, carriages, wagons, and street cars for transportation at the beginning of the twentieth century. Grandfather's business headquarters and shop were on Riberia Street in St. Augustine and over the years he owned three houses in town. Two were on Weeden Street and one on Bridge.

An interesting thing happened a few years ago. Our

family bought two houses on Weeden Street for an investment and when I went to the historical society to view their past, I discovered that the house we purchased at 64 Weeden Street was the house where my father was raised. Talk about coincidence/synchronicity!

Grandfather Faver served for years on the St. Johns County Commission and served as Chairman for one term. My grandmother was only thirty-six years old when she passed away. It was said that my Grandfather was absolutely devastated by her death. Apparently his oldest son, Uncle Hiram, was a major force in helping Grandfather through his grief and helped with the raising of his three brothers and sister. We always said this was the reason Uncle Hiram never married. He had already raised a family by the time he was twenty years old.

One of my grandfather's best friends was Doctor George Worley. When my father was born, Grandpa honored his friend by naming my father Samuel Worley Faver. The name has been passed to me and then to my second son, Kevin Worley Faver, and to his son, Worley Kolton Faver.

Doctor Worley probably saved my father's life when he was severely injured in a wagon accident. Uncle Ray was driving the horse and wagon, going too fast, and tried to make the corner, we believe, turning onto Weeden Street off of Bridge. The wagon turned over and Uncle Ray was thrown clear. Dad became tangled in the wrecked wagon, suffering head, back injuries, and severely damaging his right arm. Dr. Worley tended his wounds and visited the house on Weeden Street daily until he was out of danger.

Grandpa and Dr. Worley's favorite outing was to go on week-long hunting trips to Pellicer Creek, south of St. Augustine. How I would love to have experienced this entourage of horses, wagons, bird dogs, and hunters having too much fun.

Daddy told me how Grandpa had a favorite Model 97 Winchester 12 gauge pump with a 20 inch barrel, which he used to hunt quail. Dad said Grandpa would shoot the birds from the saddle and his dogs would retrieve the birds and bring them to his stirrup to be placed in the game bag.

Many years later Uncle Hiram purchased 800 acres on Pellicer Creek where Grandpa and Dr. Worley loved to hunt. In 1950 Uncle Hiram donated the land to the State of Florida for use as a state park in honor of Alexander Hall Faver and Florida Ellen Dykes Faver. So today, it gives us great joy to see families enjoying the place, Faver-Dykes State Park, that was special to my grandfather.

Lord, isn't it amazing how the world has changed since those days. The world's population has more than doubled. Wars are still being fought over religious differences. Technology has permeated our lives and advances more every day. We must protect the sanctity and unity of our families, because when all is said and done, love is that precious thing that will surely save us.

*

Ancient City Wagon Works Business Envelope—1904

4

PAPA GROVER

"But they that wait upon the Lord shall renew their strength; they shall mount up with wings as eagles; they shall run and not be weary; and they shall walk and not faint." Isaiah 40:31

The first time I saw him he was forty-one and I was sixteen. I sensed right away that here was a strong man, not just physically, because there was something else. Over the next fifty years I learned that the "something else" was an exceptional strength of will. He succeeded at anything he turned his mind to. The other part of his character that some people missed was his compassion. He helped people all his life with wise counsel and his resources.

Papa and I worked together as business partners for fifteen years. During that time, almost every week I watched people come to see him and pour out their troubles. He would always kindly advise and usually reach for his wallet.

The first time I saw him cry was the day I married his

oldest daughter. At that time I thought my career with Southern Bell was set, but three years later he asked me to go into business with him. That was when our lifelong friendship began. At least once a week I dream of those years when Papa and I were together every day, running the family farm and travelling to sell our livestock at the auctions.

He had an uncanny sense of judging peoples' character. He would say, "Son, you have to read their eyes. You can look into anyone's eyes and see what they are made of." He could be the most devoted friend, but he was a very capable foe if someone was dishonest in a business transaction.

When my mother left her body, Papa was not in good health at that time, but he was there when we laid Mama to rest. He said, "I owe it to you son, to be at your mother's funeral." I cannot express how much that meant to me.

Papa's health did not improve and he was admitted to a care center in St. Augustine. One day I knew he was failing when he asked me how the farm was doing. As it was, we had left the farm over twenty years before. So I told him what he needed to hear. I said, "Papa the farm is doing great, our farm hands are doing a good job and all the cows are having beautiful calves."

Another time I went to see him and he was very upset. He said, "Son, someone has stolen my wallet. All the money I had in the world is gone." Forgive me Lord, I lied again, as I said, "Papa, you don't have to worry about anything. I am so rich and have more than enough money for both of us." He smiled at these words and never asked again about the farm or money

For the next few months I visited Papa every weekend in the care center, usually taking some of his great grandchildren to see him. One Saturday one of my grandsons and I were on our way to see Papa and he said, "You know, Pops, you and I used to go see Granny Birdie before she went up. I think pretty soon Papa Grover is going up there to be with her." I replied, "Buddy I think you are right."

Then on a Saturday, I went to see Papa one last time. His voice was weak and I bent down close to his face, to hear him. He said, "Son, life is so short." I said, "Papa, it truly is, but didn't we have a good time? I sure do love you."

Then he said the last words I ever heard from him in this life, "Son, God loves us all and I love all of you." He was surely one of the most special human beings I have known in this life.

*

5

IT WILL NEVER LAST

"Love at first sight." It was a saying that I thought only really old people used, but God help me, I experienced it that day, August 24, 1953.

Walking along the beach, minding my own business, I noticed a dark-haired girl with an inner tube under her arm. What happened to my life that day is something I'll never forget. It's an old worn-out cliché, but my world did literally stop as I watched that young girl walk out of the surf wearing a one-piece, black, bathing suit.

She was   fourteen   and I was fifteen. She was a beautiful little thing, and I couldn't take my eyes off her. After introducing myself, I shook hands with her (we were polite back then), and then we didn't see each other for a couple of months. At the time, I was "going steady"— this was something we did in the fifties. But that very afternoon I told my steady girl we were done.

The courtship was complicated. She lived in west Jacksonville and was in ninth grade at John Gorrie Junior

High. I lived in Neptune Beach and attended Fletcher High School at Jacksonville Beach. Later it was obvious to me that she always had a line of boys waiting to take her on a date. At least they had impeccable taste.

In order to see her, usually Friday after school, I would catch the city bus, "52 Beaches," to Jacksonville, change buses at the station downtown and catch the "22 Lake Shore." She and her father would be waiting for me in Lake Shore. Seeing that 1952 black Chevrolet waiting when I stepped off the bus always made me happy. Friday and Saturday nights would find me in her home, sleeping with her brother.

There's an old country song by John Anderson called "Swinging," in which one line goes: "Sitting on the front porch just swingin, feeling love down to my toes." Folks, that's exactly how I felt when I was with her and come to think of it, I still do.

Sometimes we would catch the buses and meet downtown to see a movie at the Florida Theater and afterwards we would eat at Morrison's Cafeteria. We loved spending all afternoon in the great old balcony at the Florida. My memory of any of the movies we saw is very scant.

The courtship went on like this for over three years. Then one lovely, moonlit night in September, 1956, when I was nineteen and she was seventeen, we stood by the river in Ortega Park and I slipped a diamond ring on her finger. The wedding date was set for June 22, 1957, which would be ten days after her eighteenth birthday. She would have a birthday, graduate from Robert E. Lee High School, and be married all in the same month.

What a beautiful wedding it was. Our families and friends came and the church was overflowing. Reverend Joe Smith, Carl Hughes, my best man, and I were waiting to go into the church when it became obvious to me that the pastor seemed to be very nervous. When I asked if he was alright he said, "This is my first wedding and I'm scared to death." His hands were shaking so bad, he couldn't tie his tie. Telling him everything would work out fine, I tied it for him.

She was an absolute vision as she glided down the aisle on the arm of her handsome father. He became one of the very best friends I ever had, but that's another story.

The Reverend did a great job and I finally was joined to the love of my life. The reception was held at her parent's home. As we got ready to leave after the reception, her father called me outside. He handed me a hundred dollar bill —a lot of money back then — and told me to take care of his girl. It was the only time I ever saw Papa Grover cry.

Following our honeymoon, we both worked for Southern Bell. I was on the midnight to 8 a.m. shift and she worked from 8 a.m. to 5 p.m., so we looked forward to the weekends. Some weekends we would drive to Daytona Beach and stay in the Sun & Sand motel.

Our first child, a daughter, was born in 1960. We lived in a nice little house in Neptune Beach and I was still with Southern Bell working in the Central Office about five blocks from our house. The new mother would push the baby over in her stroller every afternoon to meet me when the work day was over. What sweet days those were. Then a son came next in 1961, and another son in 1966.

Now, in my seventy-ninth year, Miss Robert E. Lee is still with me and there is no way I can imagine a better incarnation. She is still the love of my life and I kept my promise to her dear old daddy when he asked me, "Son, you take care of my girl."

*

6

THE ANGEL

A certain few of us look into the face of the unknown and like what we see, but she looks into that face and embraces it. She can be the most giving and the most stubborn. She can be the most loving friend and also a very worthy opponent. And she's probably the most loyal person any of us would ever meet. Her beauty comes from deep within and touches everyone who knows her. But this is who she is at fifty-five.

Let's go back to the beginning of her path this time around. She was a first child. The parents were young and, as all new parents do, they struggled with learning how to handle this newborn child. But, between the two of them, they managed to come to grips with the demands of a new baby. There was bonding during this period, yes, and recognition even.

As she grew, it was more and more evident to everyone who loved her that she was a special child. When she was six, her grandmother retreated to a particularly dark place, but the adoration she had for this child pulled her back to the light for a while.

Watching her in those early years you would have seen a beautiful little girl who would sit in her room for hours with her Barbie dolls. She all but wore out Barbie's clothes as she would change the doll's clothing numerous times a day and in her very active imagination, she would dream up trips that Barbie would take, places she would visit, friends that she would have, and she'd arrange the doll's hair to fit the occasion. Her dolls were much more than just dolls, they were her friends.

She never had a voice lesson, but it was obvious to everyone that singing was her gift. When she began to sing, those around her always stopped what they were doing to listen. If you could have heard her sing, you would have learned what the voice of an angel sounded like. This was true music and a spiritual experience for herself and her listeners. A gift no doubt, and as we learned, not her only one.

Like her father before her and years before you would think it possible, you would find her snuggled in a deep, cushioned chair somewhere with several books around her. She'd hardly finish one before she began the next one. There was an innate hunger in her to learn about the human condition and how other people adjusted and even thrived through adversity.

She began to understand the feelings of others on a level that most of us could not approach. This was where her gift of empathy toward others had its start, and this would later serve as a vehicle for her to help others in all walks of life. As you would expect, she excelled in the classroom, especially in literature and the arts. In her adult life, many years later, we learned why she needed this knowledge and what she was preparing for.

She met the love of her life, married young, and

during those first years of marriage blessed her mother and father with three beautiful grandchildren. She spent years working for The Salvation Army, helping less fortunate people. This was no surprise. This is what she lived for.

During those early adult years, that magical singing voice matured and became even richer. Her father always said she needed to go for a recording contract in Nashville. But, singing was not her calling. Helping people would be the focus of her journey. So these days she is still a beacon of hope for many people.

Now you understand why our Angel is so loved by everyone who knows her. Her mother and father still say she was a miracle from the beginning.

*

7

THE WILD MAN

The first thing everyone notices about him is his smile. He's almost fifty four now, and that smile is still as charming as it was when he was only one. When he is really delighted by something you can pick him out in a crowd just by hearing his one-of-a-kind laugh. He was a happy child and a joy for all that knew him.

When we lived on the farm, he thought it was his own private playground. One day when things were a little slow and he needed an outlet for all his youthful energy, he invented "chicken basketball." With the help of a friend, they chased five or six hens, finally caught them, and tied their legs together.

After a meeting of their very creative minds, the two boys managed to gather all of the tied birds and take them to the peak of the steep roof of the small house where one of the farm hands lived. A bushel basket was strategically placed under the edge of the roof. After agreeing on the "rules" of the game, they gave one point to any hen that found its way into the basket after the long slide down the roof! These hens must have felt as though they were ski jumpers in the National Chicken Olympics.

Alas, the "chicken basketball" season only lasted for one game, because the referee (father) discovered the game in progress and ejected both players, to the delight of several very scared chickens.

Then there was the mini bike, purchased at the local department store. The bike was guaranteed not to exceed twelve miles per hour. After he was shown how to crank it, he rode it around the yard slowly, at what I thought was top speed. I was wrong. Later in the afternoon I looked out into the pasture and watched as a flash of blond hair zipped through a patch of dog fennels at a leisurely pace of at least thirty-five miles per hour!

Then he had a little accident one day as he tried to negotiate a quick turn, at top speed, of course, into the cattle gate. His girlfriend was riding on the back and things were going pretty well until his controlled slide carried him into a fairly large pile of cow residue, a large glob of which covered the young girl's face. He was laughing so hard, he completely lost control and crashed into the gatepost. Fortunately there were no permanent injuries. But, that may have been the last he saw of that particular girlfriend.

He is a natural with any vehicle that is fast, whether it's horses, skis, snowboards, skateboards, cars, trucks, or mini bikes.

When we sold the farm and moved to the beach he found his greatest friend in nature, the ocean. At eleven years old, he could surf with the best, and the ocean accepted him as one of her own. After many trips to the emergency room, complete with many sutures, his father filed the razor sharp edge off his skeg.

He and his friends still talk about surfing the "walls" of hurricane David. They also remember the day he caught a "nice ride" and was accompanied by a porpoise, who could match all his best moves. Now that he is an "old" surfer, he proves he still has it every year at Mal Pais.

Ah, the teenage years. Perhaps no one in our family history left such memories and survived, as he. The following incidents are just a few.

One night at a local country club, he apparently went to the second floor, and poured a large trash container of ice water on the security guard, nicknamed "10-4." No one was shot, all escaped.

His boxing career was brief, but glorious. He won his first fight against a tough little Valdosta, Georgia, kid. But he celebrated his championship and neglected his training until the rematch. Great was his fall, as he lost the rematch and went directly to the emergency room with a crushed nose. And, yes, they recognized him there.

It was Halloween. His nose was still packed with cotton from the boxing surgery, but he begged to go out with his friends to trick and treat, promising to do no damage and return home early. At 1:00 A.M. his father received the dreaded call. "This is the Neptune Beach Police Department. Do you have a son by the name of...?" The policeman was very nice. He claimed to have saved the boy's life when an irate citizen (whose house had been egged), threatened to flatten his already seriously-damaged nose.

One of the worst calls a parent can receive is when the teenager's girlfriend calls to say, "There has been an accident and we've called an ambulance." When you ask if your son is okay, she says "I don't know, he's unconscious."

Arrival at the accident scene is surreal, the crowd, the blue lights flashing, and the EMTs trying to remove your unconscious son from a totaled vehicle. They ask if you will try to remove your child, because the driver's side is crushed and the door is inoperable. So you crawl through from the passenger side, put your arms around him and start to lift, and one of those rare moments in life occurs. He opens his eyes just for a second and says, "Dad, I sure am glad you're here."

People who know him now and not then, say, "What a wonderful young man, so kind, nice, and laid back." They miss the twinkle still behind those blue eyes that his father sees. In his daily meditations, the father gives special thanks that he survived. After all, everyone knows from whom the wild-man gene comes.

Fast Forward

Well, here he is today at 55 years old and owns his own construction business with his best friend as a partner. They build college housing and small hotels nationwide. He lives in a waterfront home with his beautiful wife, but the "Wild Man" inside is alive and well. He took up road racing several years ago and has become one of the top Porsche drivers in the country. There is a popular country song playing now which says, "I have to be young and wild before I can be old and wise." This line fits The Wild Man.

*

8

THE CAPTAIN

We thought we would lose him the first year, but he survived double pneumonia. I remember watching him that first Christmas, just sitting in a chair, so sick, not really wanting to play with his new toys.

It seems like as soon as he could walk he was off to the farm every morning, wearing a tiny pair of rubber boots, and carrying his fishing pole and BB gun. The fish, birds, and snakes in the swamp took notice as he stepped into their world. This was the first meeting between nature and the Captain, and it was love at first sight for both of them.

We sold our share of the farm and prepared to move near the ocean. He didn't understand. When we left the farmhouse for the last time, he slammed the back door so hard the door glass shattered.

Once we settled in a new house close to the ocean, it didn't take him long to discover why he was there. He would always be right where he was supposed to be.

The fish in the freshwater lagoons never had a

chance. We came home one night and prepared to take a bath, but there was an eight-pound bass in the tub. It made a beautiful mount for his room.

Then he discovered the ocean and all the creatures on the shore and in the water. He wore out many little dip nets chasing fingerling mullet, whiting, and pompano. He caught far more than anyone would expect. His 20/15 vision and great hand-eye coordination helped.

We fished my old favorite spots in the Intracoastal Waterway, markers 3, 5, and especially 15. The old five-horse Johnson gave us plenty of time to view the marsh life between spots. He out-fished me pretty soon, just like he eventually out-shot and out-golfed me.

We learned much later that far before his teens, with the help of a friend, he would drag a small dinghy to the ocean at daybreak and paddle out past the breakers to do battle with kings and sharks, considerably larger than his boat. He considered it perfectly logical and pleasant to be towed toward the rising sun by the denizens of the deep. One of his friends swore never to fish in the ocean after living through one of these adventures. Of course we only learned of these escapades much later.

He was twelve when we had cattle and horses on several thousand leased acres of beautiful Florida scrub, hammock, and marsh. I would let him off at daylight on my way to the farm and pick him up on my way home at night.

He moved through this world like a Native American, seeing animals before they were aware of his presence. The places he most loved had names like Bob Cat Point, Diego Pond, and the St. Augustine Grass Patch. Oddly enough, his favorite companion when shooting turtledove was his faithful retriever, Leroy, the 250 pound Yorkshire hog.

Our cattle feed was stored in a large, old, ice vending machine which was painted yellow and had a side shed attached for hay storage. A near conversion experience was had one night while camping out in the feed house.

On a cool, cloudless night he and a friend had settled down in their sleeping bags, after a hard day of hunting. Around three o'clock in the morning, a strange humming sound awakened them. They opened the door, stepped outside and were immediately pinpointed by a blinding light from the heavens. They stared, transfixed into this light, awaiting their fate, as the humming sound grew louder and louder.

Just about the time they had accepted the fact of their apparent alien abduction, the light went out. When their eyes readjusted, they witnessed the Goodyear blimp motoring serenely away into the night. Close encounter.

Then it was time to get serious about salt-water fishing. I bought him a 17-foot johnboat with a 25-horse Johnson, thinking it would be a good starter Intracoastal boat. He pulled it with a vintage, old, Ford pickup before he was old enough for a driver's license.

Very soon we noticed loose rivets in the bottom and bow. Puzzling. I had never seen this fault in a johnboat. I understood, when I got a call from an old fishing guide friend one day. He said that he and the other guides out of Mayport saw the boy regularly off shore, fishing for kings, cobia, and sharks — whatever would bite! A daily beating in ocean chop will loosen a rivet or two.

There were other stories from this era — fighting very large swells in a small boat — fighting a large fish while your boat was sinking from losing too many rivets — and then cranking the Johnson and watching the transom squat below the surface when all the water shifted to the stern, praying the motor wouldn't quit. But the other captains and his angel would save him, wouldn't they?

I advised him to earn his college degree, get a good job and fish as a hobby because everyone knows you cannot make a living as a fishing guide. He didn't believe this apparent truth. Seemed like good advice to me.

He tried, went to the school at Sante Fe, down in Gainesville, made good grades, then quit after one semester. It was just too far from the ocean. He met his soulmate and started raising beautiful children.

Then he was on to the Gulf oil fields to captain a 100-foot, turbo-diesel crew boat. He also spent enough time a hundred miles offshore on an oil rig stand-by boat to learn true solitude and make friends with a porpoise who visited each day. But he was lonely and missed his family. So he packed up and came home.

The greatest blessing a man can have is a good woman! His woman stood beside him during the hard years and the fishing guide business they created grew beyond everyone's expectations except theirs. She was always there to encourage him to follow his bliss. Thank goodness he didn't follow his dad's advice.

Fast Forward

Well, here he is now, at almost 50 years old — one of the most sought after fishing guides in the country, turning down more charters than he can possibly do each year. He has met so many interesting people over the last thirty plus years of fishing. They invite him to their homes for hunting trips in Idaho, Kansas, Indiana, and the list goes on. He has a wonderful old hunting camp in Georgia on seventy acres and owns hunting leases on probably a 1,000 more. Behind his barn he tends eighty chestnut trees, which he says will pay for his retirement one day. Here's the lesson folks: follow your dream doing what you love, give it everything you have, find a good woman to stand by your side and success will usually find you.

*

9

FANCY

Her name was Fancy. She was a beauty, a true athlete and very feisty. Her coat of dark chestnut was stunning, as was her father, a quarter horse stud.

Having a natural instinct for herding and cutting cattle, she knew what needed to be done before the guy sitting in the saddle. In the open pasture she would start moving toward a stray before it was hardly away from the herd. In the cutting lot she was amazing, forcing cows through the gate without running over the guy closing it behind.

Some of my favorite memories are of saddling her on cold mornings. I'd swing up in the saddle and she would buck like a rodeo bronc. My old buddy, Bill Parsons, from Paris, Texas, used to say, "Worley, when God put the horn on a saddle, he did it for a reason. It's for you to hold on to when Fancy really gets rank."

Bill was a competitive roper in Texas rodeos until he almost lost a hand when it slipped into a loop in the lariat just when the calf took up the slack.

On these cold mornings when Fancy thought she was in a rodeo, I would make her run tight figure eights until she calmed herself. After that I would put her into that gentle lope that ate up the miles and, for me, was as comfortable as a rocking chair.

On nice spring mornings Fancy and I would take a long ride with lunch in the saddle bag and around noon we'd find a nice grassy, cool, spot under a live oak and eat our lunch there. I'd share my lunch with my old dog, Buck, who was my constant companion during our rides. I lost that boy to heart worms at five years old. Sadly, we didn't have really good heart worm medication back then.

On one of these rides, Fancy's right front hoof broke through the ground into a gopher hole. She immediately went down onto her right side with my leg pinned under her. I kept talking to her softly and she calmly took her time and got to her feet with me still in the saddle. Another time we were pushing the herd along the edge of the Intracoastal Waterway when a crazy old brahma cow decided she would like to swim the canal. I spurred Fancy after her and she swam around the cow and brought her back to shore. I never had to leave the saddle.

The most amazing thing that she ever did was during a roundup one fall season when we would do our branding, castrating, and worming. We were driving the herd through an open area of pasture with the marsh on one side and dense woods on the other. A lanky, old brahma-angus cow broke out running toward the woods. She had a good head start on us before I gave Fancy the reins. Fancy was never beaten in a race with any horse, and she sure wasn't going to let that cow beat her to the woods. She took off like a shot and turned the cow before she was halfway to the trees.

When we started driving the cow back to the herd, I could not believe what I saw. The area that she had just galloped through was literally covered with pine stumps sticking up four or five inches from the surface of the earth. Somehow she had managed to gallop full speed through those stumps without tripping and probably badly hurting or killing both of us. All my friends just sat in their saddles amazed.

You wonder why I love that girl so much? Rest in peace, Miss Fancy, I'll see you again one day. I still miss you.

*

Fancy

10

THE SWAMP

This may be the strangest thing that ever happened to me. It was the 1950's. During this part of my life hunting was my passion and I was hunting almost every day after school and on Saturdays. Back in those days hunting on Sunday was not an option. Sunday was the Sabbath and we all rested that day.

My favorite place to hunt was simply called "The Swamp." My family had settled in this beautiful part of North Florida over 100 years ago. My Grandfather, William Morton DeGrove, named the place "Palm Valley."

The Swamp was less than 300 acres, and had remained almost untouched. Many years later it was drained and filled to create the headquarters of the PGA Tour and the world-famous Players Club golf course. Following the construction the Golf Commissioner declared they had killed thousands of snakes during the draining and filling process. That now infamous 17th hole of the TPC is the exact location where I used to shoot squirrels and ducks.

The reason I loved to hunt in "The Swamp" was that I had it virtually all to myself. My friends and I hunted wild hogs, deer, and alligators south of the swamp in the Jamb of Sanchez, Ben Hammock, Willow Pond and The Neck, which later became the Guana Wildlife Preserve.

One cloudy, calm winter day I entered The Swamp near the Intracoastal Waterway and proceeded to hunt my way in an easterly direction toward County Road 210. It was fairly late in the afternoon, but there was still plenty of light when I came upon what appeared to be the perfect wood duck pond with lots of sweet gum and willow trees. I immediately checked the surface of the pond for ripples because on a calm day ripples almost always means that ducks are swimming somewhere in the pond. The water was calm as could be, so I settled down on the edge of the pond in some long grass looking out over a small open area with a tussock in the middle. My little Winchester, clip-fed, .22 long rifle, with a Weaver scope was ideal.

I had probably killed sixty or seventy squirrels this late in the season, all shot through the head. That's the beauty of head shots and a good scope. You either have a clean miss or a clean kill.

So I settled down in the grass hoping that some woodies would come in for an early roost. In a little while they started coming in, two or three beautiful drakes (most spectacular bird in the world), and six or seven females. They landed near the tussock, which was the ideal distance for my scope.

Knowing they would fly at the first shot, I picked out a drake and placed the crosshairs on his head. Then I fired the shot and the birds kept on feeding and preening as if they were totally unaware of my presence. After shooting three more times and missing each shot, I even tried body shots. After four shots, not a feather had been cut. Never had I missed shots that easy with my Winchester. I was in shock. Shortly, within a minute or two, the ducks flushed and flew up through the tree tops and disappeared.

Now here comes the strange part of this story. Thoughts about those birds were in my mind all week and I could not wait until Saturday afternoon to really look that pond over and try to determine what caused my misses.

Walking right to the pond would be easy, and I knew it would be no more than two or three hundred yards from County Road 210. So I walked right to the exact location of the pond. But there was no pond — it was gone. Searching the entire area carefully, I couldn't understand it. There was no evidence of a pond ever being in that area.

Now at almost eighty years old, I often think about how everyone thinks technology will eventually control nature. Folks let me tell you — Mother Nature is still in charge.

*

11

THE NECK

It was a dream come true for us. Flavian had negotiated a deal with the owner to lease the property that we called "The Neck." The land may have covered 10,000 acres including the marshlands, and the only cost to us was to build a barbed wire fence along the roads and keep trespassers off the property.

We bought about 200 head of cattle, invited a few friends to run their few cows with ours, and we were in the cattle business. We had seven or eight years before the land would be sold to the State of Florida and would become The Guana Wildlife Management Area. Thank God there will never be a house built on this beautiful place.

We bought two horses, Fancy and Mister. Flavian's horse, Mister, was a tall, lanky, sorrel gelding and my horse, Fancy, was a beautiful, deep chestnut, half quarter horse.

During our annual roundup Fancy always shined because of her cutting ability. She could cut a cow and put her through the gate better than any horse I ever saw outside of a rodeo.

Fancy was a very fast girl and we never lost a race. Many times I thought about organizing a race on the beach at low tide and inviting all comers. But somehow I never did.

One summer Fancy developed fistulous withers and a call was made to our vet, Eric. Fistulous withers is a nasty infection, apparently caused by an infected insect bite. Eric lanced the small opening, drained it, and inserted a wick to keep it from closing. I had to check the drain every day and give her a penicillin shot. Through this ordeal she never flinched. She trusted me completely and understood what needed to be done.

One cool, fall morning Flavian and I decided to take a long ride and check on the herd. What a beautiful day. Flavian, Mister, Fancy and I, along with my old dog, Buck, started out. We had our lunch in the saddle bags — Vienna sausage, saltines, and water.

About five miles south of the cow pen there was a pond of tall trees, mostly cypress and sweet gum. We named this pond the rookery, because of the countless nests in the trees where all kinds of birds were hatched and fledged. The sight we saw that morning as we rode up to the rookery is hard to forget.

The sun was just breaking the tree line in the east when we approached the rookery. As we reined in to watch the sun rise, we saw movement in the trees. A flock of ten or twelve Roseate Spoonbills rose out of the trees and when they were just between us and the rising sun, they made a turn with their wings spread.

There is no way a camera or great artist could re-create that picture, which lives in my mind to this day. The pink of those wide-spread wings against the pink and azure sky was unbelievable. Flavian said, "William, we'll never see anything like that again in this life," and we never did.

Rest in peace and God bless you my dear friend, Flavian. I will never meet a better man.

*

Great Blue Heron in the Rookery

12

THE NOTE ON THE GATE

It was almost dark when I pulled up to the cow pen gate to pick him up. He wasn't there, but a brown piece of cardboard was nailed to the gate. And I still have that note. Written in his hand with a pen the note said, "DAD: AT UNCLE MIKE'S."

I realize the world was different over forty years ago, but we raised our boys the way I was raised. From an early age they were taught the ways of the North Florida swamps and woods and were thoroughly trained in what to do and not to do with guns. I believe this is why young Southern men and women make up such a disproportionate share of our Armed Forces, because they make such damn good soldiers. Presently we have a granddaughter serving in the U.S. Air Force in Turkey who can outhunt most men I know.

My boys had complete knowledge of the animals in the woods and knew which ones could be dangerous and why. The several thousand acres on which our cattle roamed was home to eastern diamondback rattlesnakes, wild boar, bob cat, the occasional panther, and plenty of alligators.

These young boys knew what to expect from the animals. Also, they were taught to observe how the woods change as soon as the sun goes down. They saw firsthand how the animal activity in the woods at night is not the same as during the day. They learned that a whole different group of predators rule at night, and almost unexplainable events occur. When you are surrounded by fireflies and great-horned owls hooting, the imagination (or is it?) becomes very active.

Anyhow, back to the story. Many days on my way to our farm forty miles away, I would drop the boy off at the cow pen gate with his gun and lunch and wave good bye. At eleven years old he was a better woodsman and fisherman than almost any grown man I knew. These were the days before any sort of mobile telephones, so when I dropped him off I would not see or hear from him until almost dark. Sometimes he would have a friend join him and they would sleep in the cattle feed shed at the cow pen for a night or two.

So that's the reason I found the note on the gate. I was running a little late from the farm that night and Flavian had driven down to check the herd and found my son waiting at the gate. When I pulled up, the boy was eating one of my sister's delicious suppers.

*

The Note on the Gate

13

ART—VISIONS, INTENT, EXECUTION

My Thoughts on Fine Art

Very early this morning, in a dream, I met with my art dealer. We were in a room with a small group of art collectors and he and I were discussing the future of art. I told him that with all the fear and angst in the world today I believed fine art was our best hope for living life free of anxiety and stress. It is my belief that fine art was woven into the fabric of our psyches from the beginning of creation.

Fine art has historically been the remedy that has helped civilization weather change and hard times. Paintings in the caves of Europe go back at least 40,000 years. Hand-built pottery was being produced at least 8,000 years ago. Still today, this ageless work speaks to us of composure, satisfaction, and peace.

Fine art today looks toward mankind's future with

confidence and optimism. This art needs to be carefully looked at and the artist's true intent perceived in order for us to receive the complete message.

I saw a perfect example of this recently when looking at one of my favorite artist's paintings. The scene is late evening, with the moonlight shining on sky, water, and forest. If you allow yourself to enter into that landscape, you will see and feel his intent. The work is a vision, not entirely giving sharp details, but allowing us to feel/intuit the serenity, hope, and beauty of time to come. Indeed this is the future we wish for our children and grandchildren. Fine art has always been the balm for mankind's ills.

Recently I have been searching for the name of a new pottery series. From my early morning meditation sessions I have already envisioned and produced the first piece of pottery in this new series, which will be fired, and ready for a summer show. The new piece will be named "Visions" and be the first of a series of work that looks to the future.

My intent as an artist is to create unique, sculpted pottery, which elicits positive emotions in the observer, whether in the present or far into the future. My strong belief is that fine art, especially a well-made clay vessel, can have a therapeutic effect on those who see and touch it. A line from a story of my favorite epic hero, Odysseus, bears this out: **"All art is laughter to relieve us from life's griefs."**

A visit to New York City is always something to look forward to. My favorite place is the Metropolitan

Museum of Art. When I walk into the lobby and see those giant vases holding fresh cut flowers, I know it will be a special day.

My first stop in the museum is always the Egyptian section just to the right, off the lobby. Looking inside the 6,000 year old black pottery and seeing the imprints of the ancient potters' fingers is such a joy. I know how that feels.

After spending most of the day in the Met, I go down the street to the Frick Gallery. This is what I wrote in my journal after one special visit to the Frick:

"When I walked into the room I immediately felt his stare. He was a rugged man dressed in loose elegant clothing. His hands were huge and strong and you wondered how those fingers could hold a brush so delicately and produce such exquisite paintings. Then I noticed a young woman sitting at a table in a scene illuminated by light pouring through a window opposite the table. The effect of the light is miraculous as it brings the woman's face to life."

Of course, I am describing two of the magnificent paintings hanging in the Frick. The rugged looking man is a self-portrait of Rembrandt, of which he averaged at least one a year. Also, the beautiful young woman is Vermeer's creation. Art has the power to transport us away from the everyday world to a place of beautiful contemplation.

In order to survive over the millennia, man has used

art to help him through life's brutal surprises. From the prehistoric cave paintings in Lascaux, France, to the ancient pottery found in sites all over the world, it is clear that man has always looked to art for balance in his life.

Art is truly the universal language! It needs no alphabet or translation guide. It only requires the artists to intuit the gifts, which the collective unconscious stream provides, and then fashion their intent to produce works of art.

*

14

THE CLAY

The old potter sat in his studio with sunlight streaming in the broad windows behind his worktable. He thought of his life, raising children, adoring his wife of fifty-eight years, drilling for oil in the ocean, business travels to Europe and Israel, until one day he held a small piece of wet clay in his hand. The feeling of that little lump of earth changed his life forever.

For several years he studied what other artists were doing with clay and knew wheel-thrown, glazed, objects were not for him. It seemed that almost no one besides Native Americans were creating pottery the ancient way that is completely hand built without a mechanical wheel or glazes. Then one day he flew to Los Angeles on business and on the way home decided to stop off at Santa Fe, New Mexico, for a couple of days. The couple of days turned into a week as he discovered what he was looking for, Pueblo pottery.

He learned that the most famous of the Pueblo potters was Maria Martinez. She created stunning black pottery on which her husband, Julian, painted sacred symbols derived from the natural world. She never used a wheel or glazes. She used a smooth stone to hand burnish her pieces to an incredibly polished surface. Her output of work was astonishing from her youth into her eighties, and her name is now famous throughout the world. After studying her life through visiting the galleries and museums of Santa Fe for days, he decided to pay a visit to her grave located in her home pueblo of San Ildefonso.

He left Santa Fe early one morning, traveling north in search of San Ildefonso, but he had only very general directions regarding its location. He traveled back and forth on the two lane highway, which was supposed to be near the pueblo site, but could not find the dirt road leading directly into the pueblo. Finally he pulled off on the north shoulder of the road trying to decide if he needed to give up and return to Santa Fe.

Then synchronicity took over his search. He was sitting in the rental car just staring out into the desert landscape, when he noticed a faint dirt road leading into the underbrush. Then from the left side of his peripheral vision he detected movement. It was a beautiful black and white bird with a long tail. It leisurely flew in front of the car and lit on what appeared to be an old fence post with a sign attached to the top. Looking closer, some faded letters appeared. "San Ildefonso."

When he returned home he found the bird in his Audubon bird book; it was a magpie. Magpies are related to crows and have always been friendly to humans. In fact, during their famous expeditions, Lewis and Clark reported magpies would enter their tents to steal food.

He drove up the dusty little road and came upon a small village of adobe dwellings. There was a small adobe church surrounded by a low wall and there were many tombstones in the yard. Nearby stood a small building marked "Museum." He entered and found two teenagers inside. There were a few small glass display cases containing some very old "Maria" pots. He asked the children if Maria's grave was in the church yard. One of the children said her grave was in the yard but it was unmarked, according to Maria's instructions. He entered the church yard and paid his respects to the Pueblo Grandmother.

Maria was a remarkable human being. She continually supported her pueblo with her time and the money she made from selling pottery. One day a reporter asked her how much she received for a magnificent piece that is shown in a special glass case in a Santa Fe museum. Maria said, "Oh, I received a lot for that pot. I was given two shawls and forty dollars." Today the piece is priceless.

After spending days in the museums and the glorious day at San Ildefonso, studying the techniques used by these potters dating back thousands of years, the old man knew he would devote the rest of his life learning and perfecting his voice in creating pottery. He vowed never to copy the sacred Pueblo designs but create his own through meditation and visualization. He would only use their ancient techniques of coiling wet clay, polishing the surfaces, and carving his unique designs into the moist surface. The resulting pieces would reflect images from his visions, dreams, and meditation.

Almost thirty years have passed since that week in Santa Fe. In his studio working at a small worktable, coiling and shaping the clay, listening to Gregorian chants or Native American flute music, the old man produces perhaps one major piece of pottery a month. He is continually surprised by the reaction of visitors to his studio. Many of them walk through, say "beautiful work" and move on. But sometimes a visitor truly "sees" the pottery's form and design.

A perfect example of this occurred one day when a gruff, middle-aged gentleman walked into the studio quickly scanning the pieces and walked away. Within minutes he returned, took a longer look at the work, made eye-contact for the first time with the potter and softly said, "Your work really moves me." Encounters such as this inspire the old potter to continue to listen to his ancient muse.

*

Old Potter Carving the Clay

15

PANDORA

First, let me say that I am not of the human species in this incarnation. Also, I am not sure exactly <u>where</u> I am after the events of the past week. Here is what I remember of the past ten years.

Eight weeks after I was born a human woman picked me up out of my bed and said I was beautiful. I never knew my father and only dimly remember my mother, but this lovely human woman chose me and took me to her small bungalow in the woods of Palm Valley, Florida.

Within the first week I was taken to a doctor to have a small surgical procedure. The first week at my home I was allowed to wander in the yard with flowers, trees, and a manicured lawn. On my second day outside I was attacked by a large male of my species and held down in a deep bed of ferns. He was expecting something that I was unable to give after my recent surgery. So he bit my ear and I carried that little scar for the rest of my life.

I was rescued from this ordeal by a tall human male. After this rescue we were bonded forever. He always made sure I had good food and clean water. He saved my life on at least two other occasions, first when I rolled in the grass after an insecticide application and then much later when I was attacked in the woods and lost the battle to a larger and stronger animal. My wound was in the left shoulder and left a large opening exposing the muscle underneath. He patiently tended my wound and allowed me to clean it every day until it healed.

He was very careful about taking me to the doctor, because I hated having anyone touch me except him. When I would bite through their Kevlar gloves during examination and hide under the bench in the examination room, he was the only person who could reach under the bench and calm me.

We had an agreement that was worked out because we were so much alike. Neither one of us was ever fully domesticated. There was a side of him that was every bit as wild as me and he understood what I needed to be happy in this life. He would allow me to spend as much time outdoors as I wished even though he recognized the dangers involved.

Outside there was a small swamp east of the mown grass, and just south of the property was a salt marsh containing many meals for me such as mice, frogs, snakes, fiddler crabs, and fish. He accepted the fact that there was also danger for me in this environment, but he knew that I would not tolerate being kept indoors against my will. He loved me enough to let me go!

When he would go out of town on vacation to the Bahamas, New York, Santa Fe, or maybe Vermont, he would always have someone come by the bungalow every day to feed me outdoors.

One time when he planned a trip to New York I really misbehaved! When I saw him take down the large suit case from the closet, it was more than I could stand, because I did not want to see him go. So I really overreacted! I attacked him and badly bit his left wrist, so when he was in New York putting antibiotic and a bandage on his injured arm, he would think of me.

Our relationship went along this way for almost ten years. I would appear at the front door every morning and climb into his lap while he drank his Earl Gray tea and ate buttered toast. I even helped him eat his toast, because the butter tasted very nice. He would let me out every night into my wild paradise. The cold of the winter or heat of the summer never bothered me. I loved it all except the rainy season. When particularly aggressive animals entered my yard, I simply climbed onto the roof of the bungalow, where I was out of sight and smell.

This was truly an idyllic life for him and me until recently. He left for Vermont to be gone for seven days and had assigned a neighbor to feed me every day.

The first night he was gone, the unthinkable happened—it was after dark, the moon was waxing strongly, and all my senses were operating at full strength. When I stepped into the needle grass at the edge of the marsh I sensed danger, but could not determine what it was or exactly where it was, so I decided quickly to calm my curiosity and return home. By the time I reached the edge of the marsh and slipped into the palmettos and live oak trees, the danger signals were getting stronger. I considered climbing a tree and quietly hunkered down to assess the danger, but at the last minute, I decided to run for home.

This was a great mistake because I could tell that something was gaining on me. It caught me before I was half way home. He was the largest male bobcat I have ever seen and wanted to punish me for hunting in his territory. Unfortunately, in punishing me he severed the femoral artery inside my left hind leg. He left after his attack and I tried to make it home but was getting weaker and sleepier by the second and then the pain was gone.

There is a place I heard my male caregiver tell other humans about. When we are alive in this world, there is a perfect place we can only visit when we are in deep mediation. This place is where all of our happiness resides.

All the people and creatures who we unconditionally loved in this life and who left this reality all end up in a special universe and wait for our arrival so that our love can continue and bloom once again.

*

Author's Note

This story was written due to a very sad event that occurred during the writing of this little book. One of the best friends I ever had disappeared without a trace.   As of today I have marked off 32 days on my calendar since she left me.   So, for all of my readers who love animals, this is for you.

Pandora

*

16

THE ELF WHO STAYED BEHIND

He stood and watched them go. Thousands of them were moving to the distant shore, to another world, another reality. It took days for the last to pass through the portal to that other place.

In the world that the elves had called home for thousands of years, he was now left alone. It was his choice of course and his mother and father did not try to dissuade him; they understood.

Over the centuries the elves had nurtured and helped mankind achieve their present state of advancement. But in achieving, man had forgotten who was instrumental in getting them to their present level of accomplishment. Elven blood had been spilt alongside man's in the wars against evil. That same blood had mixed at times with man's to produce beautiful children of exceptional wisdom and foresight. You will recognize some of their names: Confucius, Aristotle, Mother Teresa, Plato, Michelangelo, Leonardo, Gandhi and many, many more.

The elves realized that their ancient goal was fulfilled and it was time for man to stand on his own, so they simply disappeared; all except for one.

That one had a single purpose. In his own way he would continue the fight against evil. He knew that the future success of mankind lies with their children. He dedicated his long, long life to helping man's children grow and evolve into wise, compassionate adults.

So every December 25th, he encourages his mythical status by donning the red suit and giving gifts to all of the world's children. The greatest of these gifts is love.

By now you know who he is. His name is Kris Kringle, but we call him Santa Claus. Whenever you are kind or compassionate to others, you are helping him fulfill his mission. He lives to remind us that good will ultimately conquers evil.

*

Author's Note

For many years I have written a Christmas story for my grandchildren. This is a story they particularly like and I thought others may enjoy it as well.

17

THE WAY HOME

Preface

From the beginning, certain souls were attracted to each other. In and out of universes, groups of souls swam like pods of porpoise in the collective unconscious stream, surfacing for air together and appearing for brief lives in worlds above.

> What are we?
> Where are we?
> Who are we?
> Where are we going?

As humans with this superior brain we always ask such questions. The left hemisphere, the analytical side, will always be questioning and analyzing.

Thank goodness for growing old, when the left brain slows a little and the old creative, sensual, right hemisphere comes to life. We learn it is really all right to sit an hour and just enjoy life — bird songs, a cool breeze, warm sunlight on the skin, the smell of flowers, the taste of a nice, dry, earthy wine shared with a friend — it goes on and on.

When we reach this place we begin to learn what is really important in this present incarnation. It is all about family and friends, what we truly love more than anything.

For almost thirty years I have created sculpted clay vessels from the Earth Mother's clay. This has been more satisfying than anything else I have done during this busy, adventurous life. Carving, texturing, and burnishing clay is by far the most meditative thing I have done. Those meditations pointed to the following path.

One afternoon I was sitting in my pottery studio asking myself the same question that had been on my mind for over twenty-five years. Why do Native American potters have access to such a rich heritage of symbols concerning all of plant life, animal life, and sacred ceremonial events? I had always refused to use their symbols to embellish the pottery I produced, because I believed such action would be sacrilegious.

Over the years I have become adept at using active imagination and meditation to create the forms and carvings on my pottery, but the work always felt incomplete because there was no symbolic carved imagery on my pieces. So, at almost eighty years old I decided to remedy this situation. I would try to learn to go into my unconscious mind during meditation and see what it had to say. The results were and continue to be beyond belief.

In my unconscious mind I found, through dreams and meditation, an infinite multitude of symbols which I immediately began carving on a new pottery series called "Visions." Each symbol is unique in form. I created six pieces in the "Visions" series with hundreds of the symbols carved into the walls of the vessels. These six pieces led to a major work named "Alchemy." After completing "Alchemy," it occurred to me that there was much more to these symbols than just interesting and pretty forms.

During meditation one morning around 3:00 A.M., I surmised these forms may constitute a language, so I began to try to interpret and receive the message they had for me. You cannot imagine my surprise and sense of awe when I finally began to understand the message.

Alchemists, sorcerers, mystics, and Zen masters have intuited and searched for a "universal language" for millennia. Would I be able to learn to interpret these symbols? Where would that search lead? What would my dear friends and relatives think of such a pursuit? Was I having some kind of mental crisis in my eighth decade?

I put all those negative thoughts away and directed my energy into the interpretation of the message from the other side. In retrospect I am so glad I did, because the result was beyond my wildest dreams.

The symbols have nothing to do with those characteristics we normally associate with language, i.e., no alphabet or dictionary is needed. I believe many people can understand the language if they are truly open and receptive.

When visitors came to my studio, I noticed that upon seeing the carved symbols on the "Visions" pieces they immediately began, without prompting, to say what some of the symbols meant to them.

Apparently, the symbols have the power to cause

some people to open a door to their unconscious mind and receive images and answers to questions in the observer's conscious mind.

Let me recount the event that started me on this journey twenty years ago. I was enjoying my working life and career, creating pottery at night after dinner. This is when I began truly meditating every morning from about 3 A.M. to 5 A.M., and I found that my best pottery designs came from these sessions.

My commute to work every morning took about an hour. It was a nice drive and ended as I crossed the beautiful St. Johns River, which is at least a mile wide at that point. One morning after a particular fine meditation session during the early morning hours, I was driving up the Dames Point Bridge across the St. Johns when my eyes noticed the extraordinary height of the bridge suspension towers. As my gaze traveled up the tower to the top, I experienced something unprecedented in my life. For a split second I was no longer in my vehicle but was instantly transported across the universe(s) to a place of utter happiness and tranquility.

There is no way to describe how that instant changed my life. I had seen a place beyond all pain and unhappiness and wanted to return there as soon as possible. Since that day I have been able to return there for extended periods of time.

My meditation became richer and deeper and my pottery designs continued to evolve. That was when my unconscious began sending the symbols that I had asked for in my meditations.

For twenty years my meditations and pottery creations have continued to expand in depth and complexity. Collectors began to find my work more and more interesting. The form of the symbols is sculpted directly onto the surface of my clay vessels. I never consciously know what the symbols will look like until they are carved into the clay; they are carved as they flow directly from my unconscious. I now believe that everyone has the ability to communicate in this way with their unconscious mind, although the person has to be exceptionally open to the process.

Carl Gustav Jung, the Father of Psychoanalysis, coined the word synchronicity, which describes "meaningful coincidences" in our lives happening seemingly without cause. My life has been filled with these events.

During my pottery classes over the years, I often spoke to my students about the power of clay to enrich their meditation and suggested they should not be surprised by synchronistic happenings. It has been some time since I have taught pottery, but some of my former students still contact me to recount omens and unpredictable events in their lives that point to solutions of problems in their art and lives. They say the most valuable part of my teaching was not about the vessels they created, but the deep meditations resulting from having their hands in the clay.

I recall how my mother would kneel and pray beside her bed every night of her life until she could no longer kneel at eighty eight years old. There is no way I can overestimate the impact of that daily act on my life.

When I was a child I did not want to disappoint my mother, because she prayed for me every day. No doubt, any success I have attained in this life can be largely attributed to her prayers. She has been gone from this plane now for fourteen years, but I still feel the encouragement and power of her prayers.

During my adult life I have been saved twice from certain death. The first incident was while hunting marsh hens in North Florida.

It was a rainy day and there were three of us in a small john boat. Flavian was running the little outboard and Sam was in the middle seat facing me with my Grandfather's old '97 Winchester 12-Gauge pump laying across his knees. He jacked out what he thought was all of the shells in the magazine, but there was still one in the barrel. As he pulled the trigger and tried to lower the hammer with his wet thumb, it slipped and the weapon fired. I can still feel the shot rush by my left side barely missing my midsection. I thought about Mama's prayers!

The second incident occurred in Brazil in 1986. I was Sub-Sea Engineer on a large, ocean deep-water drilling vessel. Two rough-necks and I were trying to repair a moving piece of equipment, while the rig was in drilling mode. My relief on the previous hitch had refused to work on the equipment while it was moving and in operation. The three of us were on a narrow, metal catwalk over sixty feet above the steel deck. We almost had the repair completed when a chain holding a component of the equipment slipped and the large steel piece almost fell on us. The two roughnecks dove backwards down the catwalk but I had no place to escape except open air.

As I fell backwards, I knew for certain I was a goner. But then I felt a hand in the middle of my back pushing me safely onto the catwalk. When I turned to see the "hand" that saved me, I saw that it was actually a large canvas drain hose coming from the drill floor above.

One of the badly shaken roughnecks said, "My God,

Mr. Worley, we just installed that hose last week."

Prayers and meditation coupled with love is a powerful tool.

*

18

The Meditation

Only the individual can interpret the message from their unconscious, I believe. As you read the following, you will understand how truly personal these messages can be. Thankfully, I have been able to receive and interpret the message meant for me. The result has been the most gratifying event in my life. You, dear reader, must fill in all of the pertinent information regarding your personal life on earth. I offer my personal view of this magical place simply as an example for your use.

—Assume a comfortable position, either sitting or lying down.

—Begin to notice your breathing, the rhythm of it, and the cool air entering you lungs.

—Relax your shoulders, arms and legs. When you are truly relaxed, in your mind's eye locate in your chest cavity, behind your sternum and beside the heart, an entity that has been with you since you were conceived. This tiny entity is your spirit or soul. It has no matter in

95

this universe and exists free from time and space and is capable of traversing the universe(s) instantly. Einstein's speed of light (186,400 miles per second) does not apply to it. It can appear anywhere the instant you think of a location.

—Imagine that your spirit leaves your body and hovers above you.

—Begin to see what your spirit sees. Looking down from its position above it sees your totally relaxed body sitting or lying. Your essence has transferred to reside wholly in your spirit.

—The journey begins here to a place that has existed since the universe(s) were born. Your spirit begins to move step by step to locations along the way so that you do not become disoriented.

—The first stop is in the sky above your home, perhaps you see the trees, lawn, your automobile parked in the driveway. You have become the eyes of your spirit.

—Next is a view from high above where you see rivers, the ocean, and the entire outline of your home state. In my case, I see the whole outline of the Florida peninsula, the Gulf of Mexico and the Atlantic.

—Then it's on to the surface of the moon, where you calmly watch this beautiful planet, earth, slowly turning with whole continents passing in review.

—Move out to the edge of the solar system passing by our sister planets, through the asteroid belt and looking back to see our sun only as a very bright star.

—We are positioned above a lovely sight. Our Milky Way Galaxy slowly spins below us and we know that our home is somewhere in one of those spiral arms.

—Turn around and look and there are so many galaxies they appear to be clouds of stars.

—Continuing on finds us on the edge of what is similar to the cloud of galaxies left behind. But no, all of the innumerable specks of light are universes. We have reached the edge of all there is, or have we?

So here I am at the edge of the universe(s) standing where? I look down and it is fine sand under my feet. Turning around I look into a magnificent sunrise over a beautiful ocean with waves lapping onto the beach. I hear familiar laughter. Looking up the beach a sight presents itself, which brings tears of joy to my eyes. Here comes my lovely wife with long, braided, white hair flowing over a silken gown, riding my favorite quarter horse mare, Fancy, with no need for bridle or saddle. She obeys Dena's soft whispered commands immediately.

Then there is a sight that brings even more tears. Sitting in front of Fancy giving me an indignant stare is my beloved Siamese cat, Pandora, who vanished without a trace, while I was writing this little book.

I look to the west and see that this place has all the features that I love, palm trees to the edge of the beach, a sturdy little bungalow with a porch all around, grass in the yard for Fancy to graze, mountains in the distance behind the house.

As we all walk toward the house I am amazed at who else is here on the front porch. Lying there wagging their tails are my long lost favorite dogs, Buck who came here in 1985 and Mickey who has been here since 1945.

It is time for me to leave and return to my other home. The journey reverses, from the beach, the edge of the universes, the edge of our home universe, above our Milky Way, the edge of the solar system, seeing our planet from the moon's surface, above my state of Florida, above my Palm Valley bungalow in the woods, in a room looking down at this old man in deep meditation and then entering his body to nest below his sternum and beside his heart.

I come to this place anytime I wish, simply by closing my eyes and entering into meditation. On one trip I invited my mother and father for supper. They have been waiting for me since 1981 and 2002 respectively.

What a special treat it was to break bread with my dear grandmother whom I have not seen since 1954. She was the best friend I ever had before Dena and also the only grandparent I knew. Then one special day I was able to meet those grandfathers and grandmother I never knew.

So by now you have the map of how to navigate this remarkable journey. I challenge you to imagine the details of your true home and then visit there as often as you like. As for me, when I feel my heart take its last beat or that last breath enters my lungs, you know where I will be in the next instant. This is The Way Home!

The End

Author's Final Note

During this journey of joy, heartache, pain, fortune and misfortune, there was always a constant source of love and support. As a boy I was spoiled to perfection by my grandmother and my mother. As a grown man there was a person who equaled and even surpassed their love. She was there during those years when I was following my dreams and ambition around the globe, helping and teaching our children, giving them her love and support as they became adults. She has always been the rock that our family looks to in good times and bad.

She is my soulmate and by far the better half. She is called Dena.

*

Made in the USA
Columbia, SC
05 May 2019